Through the Kaleidoscope

Poems by
Carey Link

BLUE LIGHT PRESS ◆ 1ST WORLD PUBLISHING

1ST WORLD
PUBLISHING

SAN FRANCISCO ◆ FAIRFIELD ◆ DELHI

Through the Kaleidoscope

BLUE LIGHT PRESS
www.bluelightpress.com
bluelightpress@aol.com

1ST WORLD PUBLISHING
PO Box 2211
Fairfield, IA 52556
www.1stworldpublishing.com

BOOK & COVER DESIGN
Melanie Gendron
melaniegendron999@gmail.com

AUTHOR PHOTO
Ashley Vaughn
White Rabbit Studios

FIRST EDITION

ISBN: 978-1-4218-3676-8

"I was a star falling from the night sky
I needed you to catch me."

From "Falling From the Night Sky"
— Joy Harjo

Table of Contents

Trust

With my back turned
I take a chance
on outstretched arms
and find the cradle of a bridge —
a rite of passage.

A miracle between earth and sky
sways somewhere
on the roundness of a breath.

2020 Time

In memory of Evelyn Spearman

Evie teaches Emmy to count
as their fingers rise and fall together
on opposite sides of the window —
1-2-3-4-5.

Poetry

When I write a poem,
I listen to the colors of a whisper
that rides on the shadows
of my dreams

and follow the asymmetrical revelations
of metaphors and allusions —

the circle of a prayer
born between twilight and dawn.

Infinity

I am a strand of light
living and dying
in every color ...

On a Drive in New Mexico

I touch a veil
of indigo, rose
and starlight.

Twilight by the Sea

Emerald and white turns
on the roundness of a breath.

Gulls bow and sway
in a veil of purple rose
as sky and earth merge.

Saturn

I swing-sway
through a tapestry
of arcs and hollows

where rings bloom
and bow to earth.

Confession of a Poem on Crumpled Paper

I walk sideways
through the hourglass.
To touch earth,
I am folded, shifted

by the revolutions of wheels
and a circle of hands.

Tabula Rasa

I watch the Puppeteer
as I sway behind the scrim.
Sun and moon are empty compasses.
Is Earth round?

What are colors between
black and white?

Ghosts and I
watch sugar dissolve in tea —
then try to taste the bittersweet.

Chain of Beads

Dedicated to my grandmother, Rosemary Link

She wears secrets
like a chain of beads,

leaves traces of the web
behind crevices —

a passage she never opens
and no one asks to visit.

I search for answers
in opaque blue veins
and rose-colored valleys.

She dreams
of sea salt and green.

To Walk a Frayed Tightrope

I swing over holes with my eyes closed,
glide on the roundness of a breath
and balance on the edges

of asymmetrical curves.

A Metaphor for Cancer

Cancer is a crooked road without signs,
where the ground shifts without warning,
and I swing-swerve on the edges
of its asymmetrical curves

as circles of smoke signals rise
into the arid open.

I feel betrayed by my body.
I'm not going to win.

At the Back

I sit waist-high in a wheelchair.

One revolution at a time,
you push me past the ramp
and up the gravel path
into the back door.

Solace

I find comfort
in the wings of our joined hands,
swaddled by red leaves the color of cardinals
in a labyrinth that cloisters earth and sky,
my head arched in the V of your neck.

As gold shadows ripple
I read a poem to you until the last syllable
dissolves off my tongue —
my senses, bringing the word back to me,
floating like water.

I trace the outstretched branches of your cheeks
seeking ancestry.
An after twilight swim through watercolor prisms
cradled by a silver solstice
and polyphony of crickets.

We sway on tire swings
and bathe in warm red clay,
creek bottoms.
Listening to stories beneath evergreen shade
as I stroke
the round of my dog's back.

Like my dog
solace always comes
without my asking.

My First Cradle

Before I know time
language — distance — sound …

I swim from the pendulum
of the oval house.

Wet and blue,
I float
on specks of light —

a translucent, static body
curled in a palm.

Born twelve weeks premature
at almost three pounds,
I survived near death.

In a breath
I carry
shadows.

Through the Kaleidoscope

Between the colors of my dreams,
objects float
in non-cyclical orbits,
like the round puff of a held breath.

Half moon twilight tunnels fold
at intersecting angles,
reflected in the circular arch of a back.

I walk a tightrope
with hangman and rocking horse.

Asymmetrical light sways
through the hourglass.

A mirage of water and rocks.
Shadows climb over crinkled waves of lace.
I raise my eyes toward a prism,
blurring distinctions
between heaven and earth.

You enter my room
in silhouette
and extend your hand to me.

Our two fingers cross.

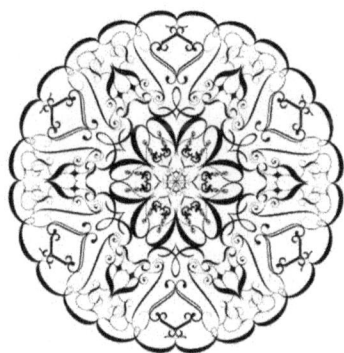

About the Author

Carey Link lives in Huntsville, Alabama. In 2008, she graduated with a B.A. in psychology from the University of Alabama, Huntsville. She is living with Cerebral Palsy. In 2017, two years after developing metastatic breast cancer, she medically retired from sixteen years working in civilian personnel and Equal Employment Opportunity as a civil servant on Redstone Arsenal.

Coping with her disabilities has taught Carey patience and gratitude. She has never stopped moving forward and is working toward an M.S. in counseling at Faulkner University. After she completes her degree, her goal is to work with clients living with life-altering illnesses or conditions.

Carey's poems have previously appeared in *Birmingham Poetry Review, Hospital Drive, Poem* and elsewhere. In 2011, her poetry sequence titled, *What it Means to Climb a Tree,* was released by Finishing Line Press and in 2017 her poetry collection, *Awakening to Holes in the Arc of Sun* (Mule on a Ferris Wheel) was awarded second place in the Alabama State Poetry Society Book of the Year contest. Carey's forthcoming chapbook, *I Walk a Frayed Tightrope Without a Safety Net,* will be released by Finishing Line Press in 2021.

Carey enjoys mentoring emerging writers with disabilities through The Handy, Uncapped Pen online program.

Acknowledgements

"Trust" — *Songs of Peace Poetry Anthology*.

"Infinity" — Huntsville Literary Association Poet's Choice chapbook.

"A Metaphor for Cancer" and "To Walk a Frayed Tightrope" are included in my forthcoming chapbook, *I Walk a Frayed Tightrope Without a Safety Net* (Finishing Line Press).

"*Tabula Rasa*" — *Awakening to Holes in the Arc of Sun* (Mule on a Ferris Wheel).

"Chain of Beads" — *Awakening to Holes in the Arc of Sun* (Mule on a Ferris Wheel), WLRH Sundial Writers Corner.

"Solace" — *Awakening to Holes in the Arc of Sun* (Mule on a Ferris Wheel), WLRH Sundial Writers Corner, *The Valley Weekly*, and the 2020 *Poetry Leaves Anthology*.

"My First Cradle" — *Limestone Dust Poetry Anthology, Awakening to Holes in the Arc of Sun* (Mule on a Ferris Wheel).

"Through the Kaleidoscope" — *Awakening to Holes in the Arc of Sun* (Mule on a Ferris Wheel).

I would like to thank Diane Frank, the Chief Editor of Blue Light Press, for her mentorship and faith in my work. I also want to thank Melanie Gendron for her cover art and fellow poets, Susan Luthur, Bonnie Roberts, and Mike Walh, for their beautiful endorsements. Finally, I thank Dr. Margaret Bibb for encouraging me to keep writing poetry.

www.ingramcontent.com/pod-product-compliance
Lightning Source LLC
Chambersburg PA
CBHW021918040426
42447CB00007B/914